All poems and images remain the ©copyright of the author, Villayat Sunkmanitu. All rights reserved. No part of this publication may be reproduced, stored in a retrieval system or transmitted in any form or by any means: electronic, mechanical, photocopying, recording or otherwise, without the prior written permission of the author.

Front cover photograph is entitled 'SnowMoon Wolf'. Available from the album 'Wolves in Scotland' in the Special Editions section on www.wolf-photography.com

Contents**Page**

What is Post Traumatic Stress Disorder (PTSD)? 4
An opinion about the words 'Paki', 'Nigger' & 'Sioux' 5
The Naming 8
Dedication 10
Foreword 11
Introduction 12
Poems
The other side of the coin 14
Funny fucker 15
Killing and fighting 17
Your rules 18
On the range 19
War is theft 20
2 minutes 21
Watching the butterfly 22
Then and now 23
A year after Northern Ireland 24
Black in Blue 26
Sacrifice of Youth 28
Forgotten Heroes 40
The Pianist 41
Silver Moon 42
Living with corruption 43
Chapter's end 45
Do you ever wonder? 47
Duty 48
Goodbye Olive 50
Fighting for some peace 55
Lobo 57
I can see you 58
Dance 58
I fought for you 59
Summer rain 60
No man's an island 61
Interpretation 62

Stigmatised mirrors 63
Valentine rose 64
Sing to the drum 65
I'm connected 65
Drop the shield 66
Cubs and friction 67
My flute 68
False hope 68
I dreamt I found you 69
The play has begun 69
Hope 70
Fighting on 70
Closing the hole 71
Unpopular questions 72
Latin moments 73
Fighting that streak of bad luck 74
What do you do when the well runs dry? 75
I want to live at no10 76
Metamorphosis 77
Welcome Gian Luka 78
On to Italy 78
Dance in the rain with me 79
Salvation 80
What do you do? 81
Does love last? 81
Who benefits from racism? 82
It gets harder to hold on 82
At one with the Ocean 83
I'm 'Special' 83

Ending thoughts 84
Also by the author 90
Way of the Wolf - other formats 90
Organisations helping UK & Allied Forces Veterans 91
Other Formats 83
Support the project 92
Notes 93

What is Post Traumatic Stress Disorder (PTSD)?

As explained by Combat Stress: *'PTSD is a complex and debilitating condition that can affect every aspect of a person's life. It is a psychological response to the experience of an event (or events) of an intensely traumatic nature. These type of events often involve a risk to life – one's own or that of one's colleagues.*

It is a condition that can affect anyone, regardless of age, gender or culture. PTSD has been known to exist since ancient times, albeit under the guise of different names.

During the First World War it was referred to as "shell shock"; as "war neurosis" during WWII; and as "combat stress reaction" during the Vietnam War. In the 1980s the term Post Traumatic Stress Disorder (PTSD) was introduced – the term we still use today.

Although PTSD was first brought to public attention by War Veterans, it can result from any number of traumatic incidents. The common denominator is exposure to a threatening event that has provoked intense fear, horror or a sense of helplessness in the individual concerned.

The sort of traumatic events that might be experienced by members of the general public include physical assault, rape, accidents or witnessing the death or injury of others – as well as natural disasters, such as earthquakes, hurricanes, tsunamis and fires.

In the case of Serving personnel, traumatic events mostly relate to the direct experience of combat, to operating in a dangerous war-zone, or to taking part in difficult and distressing peace-keeping operations.'

An opinion about the words 'Paki', 'Nigger' & 'Sioux'

I'm Asian. My family originated from India and I was born in England. I remember visiting a cousin a few years ago and was shocked when he turned to me and said, 'What's up Paki?' I told him never to use that term in front of me again. His response was that Asian youths were using the term to claim it and make it positive, just like Black people were using the term 'Nigger' to address each other.

I told him that I felt it was wrong. Our ancestors and theirs had fought many battles in the world of civil human rights to improve certain things for us in British society. One of those things was making it clear that for people to address Asians as 'Pakis' is wrong, racist and unacceptable; just as it is wrong to call a Black person a 'Nigger'.

Why would you choose to be called something that your ancestors and many civil rights activists fought so hard to stop you being called?

Why would you dishonour their sacrifice and take things backwards in the area of race relations?

Paki is a word that was spat at Asians in multi-cultural England by some White people as an abusive word. It had a tangible energy about it ... one of hatred. The word is still used by some White people in some parts of England, to convey the same energy. The correct word is 'Pakistani' and it applies only to people who are from Pakistan.

In South Dakota, USA, the people were given the name 'Sioux' by the French settlers as an insult. Many Native Americans (or First Nations people) in that area still refer to themselves in this way. If you ask knowledgeable people from the area they will tell you that they are not 'Sioux' and that their ethnic identity is Lakota, Dakota or Nakota. Their elders and educated youngsters are trying to rectify this label and assert their true identities.

We should be careful with how we choose to identify our ethnicity and never take on a negative identity imposed through racism.

The Way of the Wolf

Poetry of a Veteran

by

Villayat SnowMoon Wolf Sunkmanitu

Foreword by Dave Puller

Paperback ISBN: 9780956488527

The Naming

Dear One,

I came awake in the night after having called your spirit to me to show me its essence. I was fully in the opening of my womb and made my way to the moon lodge. I thought this odd as usually I know when this cycle comes very clearly...and this time it simply and quietly, with no pain, opened and the blood of life gave away. I was looking into what this was significant of in the calling I had made to 'see' you and was called out of the lodge by the Moon.

As I came from the lodge I was met by the Snow Moon which had a perfect circle around it, a small one, not the usual larger one I have seen many times. I had never seen this kind of visual spirit on my sister the Moon before. I recognised it immediately as the eye of the Wolf...your eye.

Standing there beneath her, in the magic of the moment, I remembered the pain in your eyes the first time we met...AND I remembered seeing the sparkle of something much different from pain there, as well. That sparkle was the Sun...its life force...its growing power. This phase of the moon is called the Snow Moon by the people of the plains because it is the time of the year, for one night, that it is the closest to the Earth that it will be in the next 365 turnings of our Earth.

The people called it the Snow Moon because the only time they saw that kind of whiteness in nature...so pristine and pure...was when the sun was shinning fully on the first snows of winter. I know this moon to be one of the bringer of radical transformation, of shift and change. It is so close to us that its powers are amplified. So what your spirit whispered to me was that this moon is you. It carries the brightness of the Sun that is in you...it carries the transformative powers you have evoked in yourself...it carries the power to bring the blood of life and creation.

It is a powerful sign...and I offer this, Snow Moon Wolf, with love and respect, to add to your basket of seeking...for your choice. It is simply an offer...and it is your right to claim what comes to you out of this story. Feel free to take what is yours and leave what is not.

I thank you for the opportunity, for the incredible shimmering night on this mountaintop...and for your friendship...

Love and respect,

WhiteEagle

Dedication

'The Way of the Wolf' is dedicated to everyone who has experienced any form of discrimination – but especially through race and mental health issues.

Being a victim can lead to stigma but mental health issues stir up the worst reactions in people. Stigma leads to being misunderstood, being excluded and isolation. The exchange of energy between friends, family and lovers become a thing of the past and all that's left is the moment and getting from one day to the next. If you're strong enough to fight your corner and cope with the unlawful treatment you end up subjected to, you end up branded as having an 'attitude problem'.

This book is also dedicated to those people that speak up against discrimination or unfair treatment of their colleagues and friends. They are rare people in an increasingly materialistic society that is governed by sheep.

The day is coming when honour will mean nothing to those in the halls of power, if indeed it means anything now. While light needs the darkness to enable recognition of the difference, those of you that value honour, truth and justice will have to stand taller and fight harder to keep those values from fading into the pages of human history.

Foreword

As Christmas 2011 approached I was looking for a present for a special friend. I was in the poetry section of Waterstones bookshop when I was drawn to a book entitled 'Words of a Wolf - Poetry of a Veteran' by Villayat 'Snowmoon-Wolf' Sunkmanitu. The front cover portrayed a picture of a wolf and a man. I opened the book and found inside poems that were mesmerising, full of passion, intensity and without pretension. These wonderful poems were augmented by black and white photographs of children, animals and landscapes. I bought two copies of this special first collection of this gifted poet, one for my friend who treasures her copy and one for me, which I also treasure.

And now the Wolf has written a second collection. 'The Way of the Wolf' continues where his first collection ended. Poems of abandonment by the system, of ignorance of love, of casual and institutional racism, of corruption and redemption fill the pages with a technique that is intense and breathtaking. From the opening poem, 'The Other Side of the Coin', to the last , 'I'm Special', the words make the reader sit up and take notice of what is being said. 'I Want to Live at No 10' tells us what a politician should be whilst 'Living with Corruption' tells us what most politicians are.

I cannot list my favourite poem in this stunning collection, you will have to find out for yourself. What I can say is that this book is brilliant. I hope you agree.

Dave Puller

Introduction

'Words of a Wolf' provided me with a way to express my feelings about living with Post Traumatic Stress Disorder (PTSD) as a Veteran in the UK.

The purpose was to raise awareness of what it's like for some of us in general ways but to also highlight the lack of care options available to Veterans at the time.

There is no evidence to suggest that things have altered that much with regards to the care of Veterans with mental health difficulties since publishing that book in January 2010.

'The Way of the Wolf' takes you back to the start but this time the focus is examining the difficulties that were faced by a Veteran whose ethnicity is South Asian. Indian to be exact. This journey tries to raise awareness of racism on both sides of the fence, the difficulties of serving in the Armed Forces as a non white and sheds some light onto issues that non white officers faced in the Metropolitan Police Force (1986 - 1989).

The journey culminates with more poetry of a spiritual nature touching on subjects that help to ease the day-to-day battle with PTSD and the subsequent isolation that the condition and stigma causes.

The connection with the Wolf runs true throughout my experiences. According to certain tribes in North America, the Wolf has the following attributes: protector, pathfinder and teacher.

Even now those roles are carried out but perhaps in more subtle ways ... without the need of physical force.

Sitting on the fence isn't healthy,

... Pick a side before you end up with splinters where it hurts

The other side of the coin

I dress in my uniform, young and proud,
Razor sharp creases, bulled boots,
Beret badge over the left eye,
Another teenager in the ATC.
51 Squadron was my first 'home'.
I walked to the bus stop
And was stopped by an elderly Asian,
'What are you doing in a white man's uniform?'
Memories of division engendered through my parents came to the fore:
Years of having white and black friends referred to as 'them';
Not being allowed to mix with Asians of different faith;
Always having to sneak off to be with my friends of other races and cultures.
I looked at the elderly Asian, my voice was quiet and respectful,
"Sir, what are you doing in a white man's country?"

Funny fucker

'You're a funny fucker aren't ya?'
Wondering what I've walked into, I don't feel like smiling much.
I gaze at the uniformed thug in front of me.
'We should never have let you fuckers in.'
Stating that I was born here wouldn't help.
It'd probably go down like a lead balloon.
'What the fuck have you lot done for this country?'
The 50s policy of importing immigrant workers comes to mind.
Rebuilding the nation after the toll World War 2 took on 'Great Britain'.
'Seriously, what have you fuckers given us?'
I contemplate the five lagers and a vindaloo crowd,
Oh and the many convenience stores that traded when theirs closed.
'You shouldn't be allowed to wear our uniforms.'
I consider the slovenly state of his.

This is a 'brother in arms' - so I turn the tables,
'I suppose we can't all be lazy fuckers like you.'
His eyes narrow and he clenches his fists.
He's about to say something.
'What ya gonna do for a brain when you lose your dick?'
He starts going red, does this mean he's 'coloured' too?
Who the hell is actually 'white' anyway and is 'white' not a colour?
'I guess you're not circumcised. You're acting like a complete prick.'

His arse leaves his chair and he advances.
I let him get to the middle of the room.
'I wouldn't - you'll get the shit kicked out of you - and end up in a cell.'

He seems to see the black and red around the two stripes,
He sits back down, giving me daggers, his fists still clenched.
'That's the problem with people like you - you can give it but not take it.'
The others are laughing at him,
Ridiculing him.
'Remember something dickhead, I took the piss out of you, not your race.'
He sits there changing shades like a Siamese fighting fish,
And starts swearing at his mates.

I turn my back on him and walk away.

Killing and fighting

They kill any sense in your head.
They kill your education.
They kill the right to decide.
And they kill the humanity in you.

You kill in the name of Allah,
You kill in the name of God,
You kill for 53 virgins,
And you, for a pint of grog.

We kill the future.
We kill communities.
We kill trust.
And, we kill innocence.

I try to fight the triggers,
I try to fight the memories,
I try to fight the pain within,
And, I try to fight their influence.

Your rules

You made ridiculous rules of engagement.
Your rules put us at risk.
Your rules allowed murderers, gangsters and drug peddlers to go free.
Your rules undermined all our efforts as the combined armed forces of this nation.
Your rules dishonoured every oath that we took before the flag.
Your agreements feathered your own nests,
And we were the collateral damage,
Expendable souls to be traded in your secret game.
Sooner or later, you will fall foul of your own rules.

On the range

I sight up,
"Ten rounds at the target in front - go on!"
A staccato of small arms fire goes off in front and around me.
"Change magazines!"
I smell the powder.
The range warden issues further instructions:
"You will walk towards your targets!"
"When I shout 'up', you will keep walking and fire two rounds".
"Walk on!"
I take a breath and centre myself.
"Up!" Crack - crack,
The target's a terrorist.
"Up!" Crack - crack,
No time for thought.
"Up!" Crack - crack,
Decisive action.
"Up!" Crack - crack,
Hesitation kills.
"Up!" Crack - crack,
Hitting your target means you might live.

War is theft

Theft of innocence
Theft of dignity
Theft of fathers
Theft of mothers
Theft of daughters
Theft of sons
Theft of love
Theft of laughter
Theft of nature
Theft of land
Theft of food
Theft of oil
Theft of gas
Theft of truth
Theft of honour
Theft of life

War is theft

2 minutes

During the 2 minutes you'll, maybe, remember some of us.
The years of silence our memories still sentence us to,
You'll forget.

The unspoken wounds that can't be seen,
Carrying the memories of service,
You won't hear.

Standing tall, we'll walk by you,
Never showing the open wounds,
That cut like knives.

2 minutes later, you'll be back to your life.
2 minutes later, we'll still be trying to make sense of ours.
2 minutes later, another November morning will be forgotten.

Watching the butterfly

Flying here and there,
Settling for a moment,
Then taking off again.

Following a whim,
Maybe a breeze,
I feel like a butterfly today.

Unable to settle,
Unable to focus,
Lost in turmoil.

Five minutes of this,
Five minutes of that,
Five minutes of something else.

Who's got the butterfly net?

Then and now

Not related by blood,
Not bound by the colour of our skin,
We don't support the same teams,
Or drink the same poison.
Just people that ended up together,
Bound by fate.

I have no brother,
And no sister.
No father,
And no mother,
Just this motley crew.

It hurt to leave,
This family of strays,
That were closer than blood.
Our lives in each other's hands,
With one common goal,
To get home again, safe.

I'm back, there is no home.

I have no brother,
And no sister.
No father,
And no mother,
Not even the motley crew.

A year after Northern Ireland

It's a year after Northern Ireland and I stand in a darkened doorway,
In a different place and a different uniform.
The game's vaguely familiar,
But the rules seem very different.
Where there was once unconditional backup - black and white,
Now there's a lot of grey.
I don't even know if we're on the same side.
I feel ostracised, untrusted.
Why do they fear the shade of my skin so much?
Why do they fear my unwillingness to twist the truth for evidence?
Why do they fear my drive to protect the vulnerable ones?
Why do they fear my ability to stick at something 'til I know I can do it?
They place the hurdles before me and I do my best to overcome them.
The hurdles get higher and the nightmares still haunt me.
The last battle rages through me in my sleeping hours,
This battle haunts my waking hours.
Friendship is a commodity here that's tightly controlled.
I'm regarded as suspicious for upholding my values.
To come to their notice I have to shine twice as much as a 'white' counterpart.
I feel like ground flesh caught between the cogs of two dangerous wheels:
The oath and the reality of carrying it out.
I'm bloodied and beaten and unsure of who I can trust,
And every shift becomes a struggle,
Then a fight for existence.

With every policeman I challenge I become more vulnerable,
But there's no one to watch my back.
And the silent threats gather in the darkness to meld with the last battle,
Torturing me,
Not allowing me any rest,
And peace is something that seems to have become unrecognisable.

Black in Blue

We who serve as black in blue,
We fall between the cracks that appear
between our culture and yours.
Welcomed but not wanted within your ranks,
A political exercise to allay the fears of the persecuted.

We who serve as black in blue,
Learn to see beyond your words and policies.
The stark truth of political expediency,
That leaves us at risk ...
For doing the job you recruited us to do.

We who serve as black in blue,
May get to a certain rung in the ladder,
If we're that lucky ...
But expect that you'll always have snipers waiting,
To pick us off before the next rung.

We who serve as black in blue,
That never hesitated to come to you ...
When you shouted 'Urgent Assistance needed now',
Suffered when you closed ranks against us.
It never was a reciprocal arrangement.

We who served as black in blue,
Sworn to serve and protect,
Irrespective of race, gender or sexual persuasion,
Or any other barrier that Society creates,
That suffered for our differences ...
At your hands.

We who served as black in blue,
That refused to be corrupted,
Maintaining the Ideals behind the oath,
That served our communities as well as yours,
Only to be hounded out by hatred inspired by racism.

We who served as black in blue with honour...
Maintain a clear conscience,
Putting your treatment of us down to experience.
You've realised though ...
You can't police the nation without us.

Sacrifice of Youth

At the age of 19 he travelled to Ireland,
To keep the Queen's peace with a gun in his hand.
He didn't stop to ponder what the task would entail.
Didn't stop to wonder whether he'd win or he'd fail.
Posted for two years to serve at the 'Hollow'.
Ignoring their jeers, his pride he did swallow.
Locked away happy memories of the two years just passed,
Locked away his emotions and got on with the task.

Caught between the devil and deep blue sea,
He could think of nicer places he wanted to be.
Saw parents pick up their bottles and stones,
Teaching their children how to break soldiers' bones.
Hearing the news, another comrade just died,
On his lap he rests his rifle and looks to the sky,
When will it end? How many more must die?
Which of us down here are living the lie?

Sat in his barracks, he lights up a smoke,
Releasing emotions, on his own tears he chokes.
Longing to return to a non-hostile zone,
Longing to return to his friends back at home.

At age 21 he left that sad land,
Flew home to England – no marching bands.
Waited in Ludlow for the Met to call.
Didn't suspect he was being set up for another fall.
He couldn't stop searching the windows and searching the doors.
Walking along, always searching the floors.
Always checking contingency plans that he played in his mind,
Not wanting to go into a bad situation blind.

He couldn't talk to people as others can,
This boy who was sent away, returning a man.
He grew up too quickly. It was down to the task.
Couldn't talk to his generation, locked his soul in a cask.
So he went to London to learn his new trade,
With his mind and his reflexes that never did fade.
With help from his instructors, he managed to pass.
He left that location to start the new task.

At age 22 he went to Cannon Row,
And there he received a serious blow.
A 'personality conflict' with the sergeant in charge,
Who was quite determined to make his life hard.
The sergeant convinced others that this lad was bad.
He tried to convince the veteran that he was going mad.
The veteran would walk around the station with a hunted look in his eye,
But he kept working hard and managed to get by.

He passed that course and joined 'E' relief,
But only the bad sergeant's reports they'd believe.
He was questioned by his inspector on this bad report.
He gave honest answers, giving him food for thought.
He worked harder than he'd ever done before,
And through perseverance he levelled the score.
Through his efforts, by the relief he was accepted,
The bad report was finally rejected.
Good arrest reports followed, what more could he ask?
The pressure eased slightly, he started enjoying the task.
Made new friends, he started enjoying life more,
Making up for Ireland, life was now better for sure?

But the nightmares lived inside him, they wouldn't give in.
The videotape kept playing but he couldn't look within.
He was blind to the reason for living this way,
Afraid of the rubber room if they got their say.
To end up sectioned was no difficult task,
His emotions were locked tighter in that now familiar cask.
All he could do now was live for the job,
He put everything into it and worked harder than the average prob.

One day an experienced officer got posted in,
Large with evil eyes, a picture of sin.
He'd walk around all cocky, giving it mouth,
'This is the way we do things down south!'
The veteran was told by a lady to watch his back,
The WPC said, 'Watch out he doesn't like blacks'.
The veteran soon found this out as the new guy played boss,
Over two incidents that occurred near Charing Cross.
The veteran found his methods really intolerable,
He found his aims most dishonourable.
Refusing to work with him, the veteran kept well clear,
He worked alone again, didn't realise the price would be dear.

Along came the day that led to his demise,
I'll tell it quite plainly, spelling no lies.
Policing a march onto a unit he was assigned,
Ignoring the evil one who was sat right behind.
Deployed from the transit upon Marble Arch,
He stood in a cordon so's to not let marchers pass.
A gent came out of the subway, his voice sounding dire,
'Officer, in the subway below, you've got a fire!'

Shouting for assistance, he went down alone,
Down the stairway, his boots echoing on stone.
To his right in the corner, he did see a bin,
Two lads stood near it, not throwing owt in.
He nicked them for a most trivial offence,
A moment later, the explosion commenced.
A slow loud explosion filled up the hall,
Flames leapt to the ceiling, menacing and tall.
Reflexes took over, he shielded them from the flames,
Contingency plans were followed, no time for games.
He got the lads safe round the corner, feeling very tense,
He kept the public away, then the nightmare commenced.

When this nightmare commenced he was aged 23,
He looked back to the bin, what did he see?
Two officers off his serial, one dark haired and tall,
The other an ex classmate, cocky, freckled and small.
One of them went over to look at the bin,
The veteran shouted, 'Don't do that it might go up again!'
He instructed them to keep the public away,
Then along came Evil Eyes and this did he say:
He asked the veteran if the two prisoners were fine,
He asked why the veteran nicked them, said, 'They'll only get a fine'.
His eyes lit up, he said, 'Wait here' and disappeared,
Two minutes later with the other two he reappeared.

Evil Eyes called the shots, a plan he'd arranged,
The veteran's mind was reeling, he must be deranged.
He didn't want any part of this right from the start,
His mind wasn't functioning, he felt far apart.
On the way to the station his mind had gone numb,
One lad said, 'We didn't do it but I suppose we'll get done'.
Evil Eyes was confident he had the upper hand,
If the veteran could talk, would they heed a probationer on monthlies with a permanent tan?
And so the dishonourable deed was done,
Perhaps it was Evil eyes idea of fun.
Walking around even cockier, giving it mouth,
'This is the way we do things down south!'

On that same night the veteran suffered a fall,
He split his head open on the corner of a wall.
Couldn't go to work, he had two weeks off sick,
Couldn't stop thinking about the lads falsely nicked.
That incident disgusted him, it just wasn't right,
He'd already made up his mind to put up a fight.
Evil eyes was watching him like a hawk,
He knew what he'd do if he decided to squawk.
On the veteran's first shift back he was working nights,
Evil Eyes placed his bet and decided to strike,
There were four internal allegations against the veteran, which he had backed,
With Freckles as witness, Evil Eyes wanted him sacked.

The inspector called the veteran, said, 'What about these allegations?'
The veteran told him about everything, he didn't believe the explanations.
So he asked the inspector to keep quiet the things they'd discussed,
He knew time was running out to find someone to trust.
He'd run out of options and had nowhere to go,
He was left only with his sergeant, so he started the show.
His version went up the ladder to CIB,
Where he made a full statement over biscuits and tea.

The interview lasted a good part of the day,
Evil Eyes' allegations were repeated that 1st day of May.
He felt relieved when the interview was finally ended,
Only to be crushed, when told, 'You're now suspended.'
They took out the veterans words relating to the explosion,
Took out the words about Northern Ireland, they'd had a notion.
When he questioned why it had been removed,
CIB said, 'It's not relevant', but he wasn't soothed.

Suspension isn't pleasant and life becomes hard,
You seem free but you're restricted, when the Met's marked your card.
At every opportunity he'd get drunk then depressed,
All eyes in the house were watching him, he was being assessed.
His inspector talked to all the officers on his relief, said, 'Keep away from him',
The veteran had only told the truth but to them it was a sin.
Any chance to talk to someone on his relief he would seize,
Only to be ignored as if he had some deadly disease.

Blanketed in uncertainty, he was hanging on a string,
He didn't know what was going on, he didn't know a thing.
A life-threatening letter to him had been sent,
By some copper who was obviously bent.
He was moved from Trenchard to a different house,
There he minded his own business, he was quiet as a mouse.
But it didn't take long for word to get round,
Due to unforeseen circumstances, he'd once more been found.

And so the word was put out again,
'Watch him, he's dodgy!' he'd committed that sin.
The price for his honesty was in truth a great cost,
Many good friends and acquaintances he'd lost.
A spotty detective with a face full of acne,
Said, 'Watch out boys, he's a treacherous paki!'
Helplessly flung into a deep dark depression,
His only release was to get drunk, session after session.
He couldn't counter the loneliness or counter the pain,
Exercise and alcohol kept him just sane.

At Rochester Row he was served a summons for court,
He cursed as he realised there was another battle to be fought.
To have a good brief he thought was a must,
His was supplied by the federation, who could he trust?
The brief didn't want the case right from the start,
But there was easy money to be made, so he played his part.
Two years later a court date was set,
At the Old Bailey, the veteran against the Met.

Counsel said, 'A plea of guilty is your only way.'
He felt crushed again, they wouldn't listen to what he had to say.
And so the day for pleas had come,
He thought 'Damn it, just get the job done!'
Counsel said the CP won't deal, he doesn't want to know.'
They wanted four heads not three, for a convenient show.
More pressure was put on again, they pointed and said he'd committed that sin.
Officers who were friends were quite clearly informed, 'Keep away from him'.

Come the time of the trial he nearly went spare,
When he discovered that neither of his counsel were there.
The veteran had pleaded guilty against his will,
He'd been fed to the lions and they'd have their fill.
What an ordeal, eight hours in the box,
But he stood up to it and took all the knocks.
He listened to a sergeant and the kind words he'd said,
Those words gave him courage to hold up his head.
When his cross-examination was over, he felt such relief,
All the questions and emotions strained him beyond belief.

He protected the other officers that he knew,
The knowledge about their behaviour he didn't spew.
Evil eyes had involved him in this against his will,
The after effects of the explosion were a hefty bill.
Home to Leicester after the trial he was sent,
To be called back to court when his mitigation commenced.
Without prior knowledge, his police records were used,
His inspector and super their positions did abuse.
Even though they'd written good things on the veteran's reports,
His inspector and super lied about him to the court.

Three days later came the moment of truth,
The event that would conclude this Sacrifice of Youth.
Hanging on a string, he was sat outside the dock,
His heart was thumping through his chest, knock after knock.
The spokesman of the jury for the verdict was asked,
All three other officers were found guilty, that concluded his task.
As for the mitigation, he wasn't pleased with the content.
His mind was screaming. 'You're going down!' and to prison he was sent.

Taken to Pentonville and banged up in a cell,
His mind rebelling against the injustice but who could he tell?
He thought about Evil Eyes and of the cost,
Because of Evil Eyes' ego four careers were tossed.
There was shock in the community when the veteran was caged,
They all felt that an injustice had been played.
But he was a lawman, he'd taken an oath, to do his duty regardless of cost.
To protect and serve the public was his path, a path now lost.

Six years later the final piece of the jigsaw was found,
The reason for his inability to stand his ground.
It went back to Northern Ireland and an exploding bin,
An incident whilst out shopping, this scene he had seen,
A bin still smoking, people and blood,
Bodies lying because of differences in their God.
It was there for all the knowing to see,
That the Veteran went to prison because he had PTSD.

Forgotten Heroes

After the silence,
After the stillness,
After the lonely bugle has sounded.

After the march-past,
After the memories,
After the door to those feelings close.

They won't remember,
In the halls of power,
Behind their guarded mansion walls.

That without your courage,
They would have nothing,
You who protected their lands.

Whether you're in a cell,
Or cardboard boxes,
Or the prison of an emotional hell.

Hold your head up,
Wherever this day finds you,
We remember your sacrifice.

The Pianist

The notes resonate,
Vibrations surfing the air,
As your fingers glide over ebony and white.
Chords pulling on my senses,
Echoing my emotions,
Mixed up - then clear.
Your tunes soothe me,
Allowing me a few moments of peace.

Silver Moon

Silver moon, silver moon,
Can you hear my soul howl?
Can you feel my longing to bathe in your light?
I miss the way you make the waves climb the cliffs,
I miss the waves that rise in your presence,
The way that you light up the night.
You always make me smile when I see you,
You always fill me with awe,
Making me wish that I could reach you.
When I see you whole,
I know things will be ok for a little while.

Living with corruption

I see the lies they tell to pacify us,
I see the scenes that play in the background,
I see the rat race for what it is,
As I get older I see the truth,
Piecing together the whole story.
The lies they tell to create outrage.
The lies that control us.
The extension of slavery,
Now with better rewards and open to all races.

I see law officers that fear those in power,
I see judges that want to stay in the 'club'.
I see how the weak have taken over,
The corrupt pen is mightier than the just sword.
When I look at you, I wonder what you'd do,
If you were forced to decide between honour and a lie.
Could you forsake a friend to save your job?
Most do.
The strong are few, the just, less.

Power corrupts the corruptible,
Power empowers the selfless,
Power can make a difference,
If properly wielded.
How many people in the halls of power do you trust?
Would they stand on an issue and risk their comfort?
The ones that do often lose their power,
For breaking silence is a sin,
Going against the club is unforgivable.

How do I prepare my children for this world?
How do I strengthen them for their paths?
How do I teach them to manoeuvre around the corruption?
Everything changes and evolves,
For now the pen will stay mighty,
Until its circle is complete.
What will happen in the next cycle of the sword?
Will our young become what society needs?
Or will they send us closer to our doom?

Chapter's End

One day you'll go, as will I,
To the next journey.
What will your last thoughts be?
Will you worry about the things you couldn't accomplish?
Will you accept that you did your best?
Do you see death as the end,
Or just another beginning?

Some people always have a bad opinion,
Probably have one about you.
There's no point paying heed to them though,
Their footsteps don't come near yours.
They're in a society without much original thought,
Slogging through their own ant like existence.
Enjoy the next journey.

You want proof of the after-life?
You want the science?
Look what happens around you,
Everything that dies gets used up again somehow.
Humans, other animals, rocks, water and the fire in the Earth.
In some ways you live on,
As part of something larger or something different.

Have you never felt the magic in the eagle feather,
Or the fur of the wolf,
Felt the energy of a lava flow,
The vibration in a glacier?
Have you never felt the energy of the soil in your hands?
Everything goes back to the Earth, sooner or later,
And lives on in a different way.

The way we perceive death isn't the way death perceives us,
It's just another chapter in a bigger story.

Do you ever wonder?

Do you ever wonder if your words are really heard and whether they mean anything to someone else?

Whether in the chaos that continues to break down society and its values, your words can have some effect? What could that effect be? What are the ranges of the ripples that we cast forth with our words?

Are our words enough to arrest the decline in morals or do they have to be underlined by blood, sweat and tears?

Is it a fact that the audience will already understand, leaving us to preach to the converted, while those that really need to heed the words continue to walk by us in ignorance as they cast more cyclones about them to sap the strength, the goodness, the warmth, the love and the honour out of society?

Do we give in to the decline or do we continue to stand for the values that we uphold?

Will you continue to fight for what's right?

Duty

Sometimes the anger burns inside me,
Raging like a heated tornado,
Held in check ... just,
Chained by the disciplined mind.

Sometimes it leaks out,
At someone pushing my triggers.
A warning growl escapes my throat,
Fire in my eyes.

If you show me calm and civility,
You shall receive the same.
If you're trying to hurt or upset me,
What do you think I'm going to do?

So I keep myself locked away,
More for your sake than mine.
My world is harsher than yours.
There are no half measures.

My world has black & white,
There are no shades of grey.
My world is war or peace,
For I'm not a politician.

You trained me to live this way,
Acting on instinct.
Suppressing the threat.
Covering your arse at the risk of losing mine.

Politics always has to play a part in yours,
Grey words in the hall of shadows.
I don't think that way,
For there is no honour in your halls.

You bent me to your will to do the job,
But left me alone in ignorance of my wound.
Dying slowly as the knives cut my soul,
I did my duty by you ... but you failed in your duty to me.

Goodbye Olive

Goodbye Olive!
Your anger has no place with me.
You need to go and cleanse your soul.
You walked away from us,
A place of security and trust ...
That you abused.
Yet you labelled me the abuser,
Casting lies to protect yourself from your issues.
Lies allowing you to avoid facing yourself ...
And avoiding trying to heal your self.
You were the solo element in the 'family',
Focussed only on your career.
You broke the oath we gave to each other,
To put the needs of our family first.

You didn't respect me as a partner,
You didn't tell your parents we were together,
As you stood there pregnant with our son.
The man who gave up the life he was building to support you both.
Who stood by you, straddling the chasm you created that day.
I knew then you weren't strong enough to be with me,
But I stayed for my unborn son.
Caring for him, feeling real love and kinship.
I challenged my family when they spoke ill of you,
Their acceptance of you was demanded,
But you couldn't do the same with your father.
You preached 'Equal Opportunities' at work but never lived it,
Your lack of action and courage hurting your partner and your son.

You withdrew into your illness after birth,
Intimacy was no longer a consideration,
Refusing to acknowledge something was wrong,
Even though I was getting my PTSD treated - for the good of the family.
You betrayed everything that we had built up.
I was surprised when you agreed to try for a sibling for our son.
A difficult birth that nearly claimed you and our daughter.
I felt no love for you but I reached out to you,
Rescuing the spirit of the mother,
And in doing so, rescued my daughter.
You then withdrew completely from me,
Unable to function as a partner or mother.

I had taken our family back to the Ocean.
Back to a place of beauty and clean energy.
It wasn't enough for you though and the chasm widened.
You found being a mother difficult.
It wasn't a role that you committed to, complaining often.
Always seeking to put the blame of your unhappiness at my feet,
Rather than having the courage to get treatment for your affliction.
You kept threatening to self-harm,
Kept trying to manipulate me with passive aggressive comments,
Trying to drive me under as I worked hard to feed my family and serve the community.
I stayed with you for the good of the children,
Putting up with your manipulative behaviour,
Knowing that the end of 'us' was approaching.

You wanted to go back to work and I found a way for you to do it,
But it wasn't enough.
I agreed to look after our children and to do different work,
Allowing you to be free once they were both being schooled.
But you broke the agreement and brought more stress to the home,
Nothing was good enough for you.
You eventually left, taking my family with you.
One year and three men later, you wanted me to take you back,
Having dumped the failed relationship at my feet.
Twelve months it took for me to see what had happened,
To value myself again.
I refused to take you back and your anger was colossal,
And your anger was forged, honed and has been aimed at me since.

You neglected our children,
Leaving them locked in strangers' homes while you fornicated upstairs,
Leaving them frightened in case their talk angered your bed mate.
Yet you always preached about my lack of responsibility,
Defined by your flexible dictionary.
I sometimes wonder how things would have turned out,
Had the truth been known about your actions,
But that would mean harvesting something negative inside of me,
I'd rather steer clear of such practices,
Even as you pressed the triggers of my disability,
Purposely trying to get a reaction out of me.
The wall of discipline held,
Even under extreme provocation.

You found another man and married him but saved your anger for me,
Inconveniencing me where you could,
Always putting your family's needs before mine re our children.
You dragged me kicking into your circle of hatred.
A place that I had stayed clear of.
You stopped my extra time with my children,
Ridiculed my name,
Spread untruths about me and exaggerated things that happened;
Anything to paint me in a bad light.
You made me say goodbye to my home, the ocean and my children.
You took away that which was sustaining me and poisoned young minds,
As well as older ones, against me.
But you couldn't completely sever the bond between the father and cubs.

I wished you luck when you married, having no anger toward you.
Hoping that your anger and bitterness would dissolve in your union.
I visited your home when the children were being difficult,
Made them listen to you and your man,
Instructing them both to obey and respect you both,
While you ridiculed me behind my back,
Trying to poison others against me.
I gave you healing,
I gave your husband healing,
You always took with a smile,
But then would send more anger.
You took advantage of my sense of honour, my vulnerability,
You took advantage of my honour, my disability.

I never loved you and I don't hate you.
I stayed with you for our son and then our daughter.
I treated you fairly or you wouldn't have tried to come back.
You found out what you'd lost and tried to reclaim it,
But you didn't succeed.
You always preach at me about responsibility,
I spent my life working responsibly,
Risking my all to always do the right thing,
Something that you've yet to do.
I don't hate anything in this life,
Not even the terrorists I went up against,
But if I were to hate anything,
Your actions would justify you being the recipient of it.

So get out of the past.
Resolve the issues you have with your father,
Leave what we had together in the past as it was over a long time ago,
Keep the kids healthy and stop using them as weapons for mental warfare.
They're old enough to see what you're doing now,
And will soon be old enough to come and visit me when they want.
Above all recognise your role as the abuser in this scenario,
and seek some help before you end up in a rubber room.
Enjoy your present,
Enjoy the children,
Enjoy the time with your new man.
Live a good, happy life,
And stay out of mine.

Fighting for some peace

The soft tones dilute the noise in my mind,
Breaking the never-ending cycle of thoughts,
Bringing some peace and quiet,
Bringing some rest.

I sometimes wished I worked on batteries or mains,
I could at least turn myself off now and then,
Allowing things to wind down,
I need a break.

I don't want to look for a rifleman in a city window,
Or a tripwire in a farmer's field,
Don't want to feel the threat,
The advance warning.

I don't want to keep playing the contingency video,
Building in adaptations to new scenarios,
But you keep me on full alert,
You keep me on the outside.

You don't try to understand where I've been or why,
You don't know about the dangers at your door,
Or the job I chose to do,
Perhaps you never will.

You'll drop some money in a box somewhere,
You'll wear your poppy for a few days,
You'll nod your head in disgust,
At the misfortune of a veteran.

To most of you we're boys that played with guns,
And beat our chests to prove we're men,
I was misunderstood then,
I'm beyond your ken.

So here I sit on my own in a darkened room,
Trying to stop the noise for a while,
Fighting within myself,
For some peace.

Lobo

Lobo whines gently,
Calling me back to the family I once knew,
Her eyes see my core,
My scars,
My pain ...
And my light.

She surrounds me and comforts me,
Nibbles the hair on the back of my neck,
Smoothes my scars,
Eases my pain,
Adds to my light.

She jumps up behind me,
Stands alongside me,
And in those moments...
There are no scars,
There is no pain,
She is my light.

I can see you

I can see you when I close my eyes,
But I don't remember your face.
I could walk past you tomorrow and never know you.
Your scent lines my every breath,
Keeping me alive but lost in my waking hours.
Your eyes hold me close to your soul,
Protecting me,
Keeping alive the promise that you're coming to me,
As quickly as you can.

Dance

I remember the warmth of your hands in mine as we moved together,
Your eyes showed me a soul alive with the music,
Enjoying the freedom it provided.
Moving together as one as I felt alive in the glow of your smile,
Our bodies in tune...

...Then you disappeared.

I fought for you

I battled for your rights,
Focusing the dark churning energy within.
Energy borne of injustices suffered.
I fought their darkness with mine,
Two minuses making a plus.
Hitting them with their tactics,
But always within the letter of the law;
Something they always used to take rather than give.
Seeing myself in some of the clients I represented,
Knowing there was something wrong within me,
Afraid to explore it through fear.
Fear of sliding down that slippery slope.
I never backed down from the fight,
Placing myself before those that wrought injustice upon you.
I did my duty by the silent oath,
Words that left a resonance in my soul from earlier life.
The fight allowed me to hide from my ailment,
Your problems becoming my diversions.
Fighting the twinset and pearl brigade within,
Those who didn't approve of a working class manager.
Fighting the privileged few on policy,
Making them aware of your reality,
Of poverty,
Of racism,
Of sexism,
Of disability discrimination,
Of homophobia.
You helped me to process my darkness.

Summer Rain

Summer rain cooling my skin,
Tiny rivulets reviving me,
Cleaning away the stain of modern life.
Making ripples wherever I look,
In the water,
On faces as they smile at the man-child all wet.

Summer rain washing my soul,
Carrying away the stress,
Setting me free for a while.
Happily splashing in puddles,
Soaking me to my skin,
Helping me to face another day.

No man's an island

No man's an island they say,
Yet they make me live as one.
While the media hype surrounds me with false promises,
I see the reality - still misunderstood,
Still ostracised,
Still unsupported.
The courage that it took to expose my wounds to get the help is almost depleted,
Survival demands that I shut down again.
Close down and hide the pain.
Close down and not seek help from those that don't really understand.
Close down and allow myself some dignity instead of constant probing.
Close down and ignore the questions...
And the isolation that follows.
Close down and fade back into the grey,
And not allow them to use my life as a lie saying they really care about us.

Interpretation

Listening to the drum,
Slowing my heart to that beat.
The chants fill my senses,
I understand without knowing.
Feeling the power of the song,
The love of the singer.
For the moment,
All is well.

Stigmatised mirrors

We're calm until you upset us.
We get upset when you don't do your job well.
We get upset when you treat us unfairly.
We get upset when you don't take responsibility for your actions.
We react to you in equal measure, physically or otherwise.
We never start the problem,
We're just trying to exist in a society that doesn't want us.
We're not violent by nature, it was just a skill of the job.
We only use it when we're threatened.

So the next time you end up with one of us having a go at you,
Ask yourself why you caused the reaction.
We can manage our disabilities within ourselves,
It's only your lack of manners that causes problems,
Or your lack of regard for this person that you're 'assisting'.

We can be placid,
We try to control ourselves and keep the craziness at bay,
We are normally well mannered and very caring,
We can empathise with your position,
We can help you to help us,
We keep away from you during our worst moments,
We still try and do the 'right thing',
We are still very capable in some ways,
We accept our limitations in others.

You just need to stop pissing us off.
You need to stop stigmatising us to justify your behaviour.
You need to face your fear of us.
You need to discriminate less and be more inclusive,
Especially as we ended up this way while protecting you.

Stop dumping your crap at our door.

Valentine rose

Give a woman a Valentine's Day rose and you feed the material machine.
Give a woman a rose bush and a trowel
And they'll both grow.

Sing to the Drum

Dhummm, dhummm, dhummm, dhummm,
Feel the beat of the drum,
Hear the song,
Ancient and new,
The heartbeat of the Earth lies there.
Empty your mind of all else,
Connect to her beat,
Sing the ancient song in your heart.

I'm Connected

When I put in something of myself,
When I look and I can see,
When I touch and can feel,
When I respect a stone,
Or some clay,
Or a leaf,
Or a cone,
When I respect myself - I'm connected.

Drop the Shield

You've got a fence and it's keeping me in pain.
The same pain you're locking yourself in.
The shield around your heart blocks out any warmth.
Let it down for me and let me in?
Let me drink in the beauty that is you?
And let me feed you with my love too?
Let me take your hand in mine and walk across a meadow?
Let me feel the sun shine on us both?
Let me watch you smile at some little miracle of nature?
And let me swim in the waters of your soul?

Cubs and friction

She can only hurt me through my cubs.
Passive aggressive tactics twisting their young minds,
Damaging their tender spirits,
Causing vulnerabilities instead of strengthening them for their journeys.
Everything I taught them withers away under her bitterness.

I step back to give my cubs space,
Taking some of the friction out of the equation,
Trusting that that they'll learn to see things for themselves,
That our bond will survive,
That they won't forget the lessons learnt by the beat of the drum.

I see their pain and frustration,
I remember when those emotions weren't a part of their persona,
When her anger hadn't consumed her,
Before she started lashing out with tongues of fire,
When she realised that I wouldn't take her back.

My flute

The sound sends me,
Many miles away.
Over mountains,
Through trees,
Back to a life I knew.
The freedom completes me,
Chains fall away.
I feel energised.
I feel alive!

False hope

A smile, a date and more,
Time taken to explore each other.
A bubble created where reality ceases to exist.

An individual desire comes to the fore,
The bubble bursts.
Hope disappears.

I dreamt I found you

I dreamt I found you the other night,
That everything was good,
That we were happy.
You didn't hide me from your parents,
You weren't affected by the shade of my skin.
You were strong and beautiful,
And you gave me that which I have been waiting for.

The play has begun

In the darkness our bodies entwine,
Shadows play across us,
Masking points of pleasure,
Reactions gauged by soft moans,
And gentle sighs.
The play has begun.

Hope

Feel the warmth from your core,
Your life force.
Open yourself to the connection,
To the unexplained.
Let suspicion fall away,
Find hope in your warmth
And dare to feel the warmth of another.

Fighting on

In the silence, tears fall.
Washing out the pain.
Making room for the struggle of another day.

Closing the hole

A darkness so deep existed within,
Denying happiness, warmth and love,
Born of troubled times,
It stretched out like black ivy,
Clinging to my being,
Suffocating me.

I reached within today and sealed the chasm.
I reached in today and found the child,
Making him laugh as I tickled him and he laughed.
I held him close and loved him,
Glowing in the smile that he returned,
Warm in the understanding that we're both loved.

Unpopular questions

Who created the creator?
Why do I have more hair in my ears now?
Did Thatcherism bring about the downfall of Great Britain?
Can corks stop dysentery?
Why is suicide frowned upon?
What's Veet?
Whatever happened to manners?
Is a shag out of the question then?
Did any deity say it was okay to kill for oil?
Have you got a headache tonight?
Why are paedophiles that are religious officials protected?
Are haemorrhoids compulsory?
Did some Americans fund terrorism in Northern Ireland?
Was that a creak or a fart?
Is our 'reality' someone else's dream?
Is it hygienic to remove bogies from your nose?
Was there collusion between the government and terrorists during the 'Troubles'?
Have you ever taken a bribe?
Which hand do you eat, shake hands and wipe your arse with?
Did France stay out of Iraq because of an oil deal?
Was Izal just a smear campaign?
Why is euthanasia wrong?
Do you need Viagra love?
If we're so well educated, why do we still have wars?

Latin moments

Her eyes twinkle,
She smiles,
Her gaze holds me,
And I feel the connection.
The Latin beat moves us,
The crowd doesn't exist,
There's just us.
My touch is gentle,
Subtle but sure,
Not all can follow it,
As it should be.
I exist within the song,
Within her eyes,
And her smile,
Lost and free.
She moves in closer,
We sway together,
Nothing's found,
All that was is lost.
Minutes of perfection,
No deception exists,
We only have the time of the song,
The dance becomes salvation.

Fighting that streak of bad luck

I found it started a long time ago,
Things went wrong from an early age.
I always fought on,
Always tried harder to get where I wanted to be.
Always trying to break that streak.

I found brothers in arms,
Closer than brothers of the same blood,
They drifted away in civvy street,
Always missing them and the times we shared,
Always thinking about them and hoping they're safe.

I found brothers and sisters,
Not all stayed close to me,
But I always carried on,
Always trying to replace those missing parts of me,
Always ignoring the pain of experiences past.

I found mothers and fathers,
They took this stray in for a while,
But I couldn't adapt to them,
Always trying to move forward,
Always dodging tentacles of the past.

I found lovers on rare occasions,
For a while I found solace with them,
But things went wrong as the streak reappeared,
I still try to move forward,
I still keep my heart open.

I need to break that streak of bad luck.

What do you do when the well runs dry?

What do you do when the well runs dry?
What do you do when the hollow overtakes you?
Lost, floating, no soul in sight.

What do you do when every road leads to a dead end?
What do you do when there's no satnav for your road?
Every right turn's a wrong turn.

What do you do when trying hurts?
What do you do when light won't penetrate the dark?
Swimming close to the waterfalls edge.

What do you do when the well runs dry?

I want to live at no 10

I want to live at no 10,
I want to do that job,
Don't want paying for it,
Just want to put things right

I want to bring back decency.
Teach people what honour is.
Keep our troops out of unnecessary fights.
Get kids some discipline

I want our people to rise together,
Instead of climbing over each other.
I want the corruption reduced.
I want community spirit revived.

I want politicians taken off pay,
Doing that job should be a privilege.
I want directors without bonuses,
A fair wage for all.

I want discrimination lessened,
Discrimination awareness to be part of the curriculum.
I want ignorance reduced,
I want people to open their eyes.

I want to put the humanity back into humans.
I want children to be safe in our streets.
I want elders to be cared for.
I want you to feel this is your home.

I want real peace.

Metamorphosis

I crouch on my tarmac jungle,
The sunlight warms me right through,
Energising me,
Minimising the pain.
My hands dig into the earth as it rains,
Forming dark liquid pearls racing toward the soil.
I seek the rainbow but see none.
The winged ones chirp their curiosity at me,
Making me smile as I watch their antics.
Colours swim in my eyes,
Bringing light to the shadows in my soul,
The scents of nature reviving me.
I smile from deep within as I watch my garden come to life.

Welcome Gian Luka

A new breath,
A new life.
The warm embrace of a new mother,
Tears of a new loving father.
The circle of love widens.
Welcome Gian Luka.

On to Italy

Another grey day on the runway,
Rain and snow alternately fall.
Wings need to be de-iced,
Allowing us the freedom to escape.
The vibration is more than usual,
Becoming worse as we rotate,
Then we're free!
Bumping our way through the clouds,
Blue skies appear,
The air is calmer.
The chains of the rat race fall away,
People are chatting, laughing,
On to Italy!

Dance in the rain with me

We are the same in so many ways,
Parallel paths creating similar scars.
The pain we hide from prying eyes,
The facade that we present.
Some would say we live a lie,
But we are survivors despite our ordeals.

You honour me with your truth and openness,
I will do the same.
For the real challenge is finding an open, accepting heart that understands.
One that can listen without judging,
That can feel in ways other than sympathy.
That can live in the moment.

So dance in the rain with me,
Even though you're not here.
Splash in the puddles and look up to the clouds,
Embrace the freedom of the moment.
Let your heart be free sweet angel,
And dance in the rain with me.

Salvation

The plants and the birds are my relations,
Beings that I share space and time with,
Neither encroaching on the other's emotions,
All respectful of each other's space.
Grandfather Sun warms my back,
Easing the physical pain,
Mother Earth grounds me,
Reminding me I am connected and cared for.
I watch for buds, chicks and tadpoles,
I'm caught up in a calendar without words or numbers,
My eyes and my senses are my guides.
Six-legged beings get my attention,
I marvel at how bees can fly - especially when loaded!
I wait patiently every year for the first newts,
And the first dragonflies.
My garden is my salvation.

What do you do?

What do you do when the sun can't shine on you?
What do you do when you can't breathe?
What do you do when the ties are all severed?
What do you do when there's no one at home?
What do you do when your words fall on deaf ears?
What do you do when you've become invisible?
What do you do when the barrier's too high?
What do you do?

Does love last?

It seems to come quickly,
Intense like a hot fire,
Cleansing everything.
Then it burns low,
Eradicating itself,
Leaving a hollow behind it.
Doesn't sound like love off the TV set.

Who benefits from racism?

Paki, nigger, wop, dago, chinky,
Divisions created through ignorance and hatred.
Words engendering sectarianism without cause,
Facilitating 'divide & conquer'.
Breeding more racism in souls unprepared,
Teaching youngsters to look for differences,
Ignoring commonalities.
Who does racism serve?
Who benefits from 'divide & conquer'?
Think on this before contributing to the circle of hatred.

It gets harder to hold on

Every new bad situation piles up,
Negotiation through the Pain field becomes difficult,
Senses are numbed.

At one with the Ocean

I ran in her presence,
Floated in her essence,
Listened to her lullaby,
Witnessed her power,
Drifted in her caress.
She's now a million miles away,
But lives in my soul daily.

I'm 'Special'

I'm 'Special'.
I have a weird sense of humour,
I rarely conform to the crowd,
Preferring the company of people to sheeple.
I'll tell people what I really think,
Rather than what they want to hear.
I find humour in silly things,
Like making human bubbles in the bath.
I can see beyond the bullshit.
Yet the label isn't flattery,
More a confirmation of being different.

Ending thoughts

To the Veteran

If you have this condition, PTSD, my heart goes out to you.

We were conditioned to survive and carry on, no matter what the circumstances that we found ourselves in. It's that conditioning that allows us to fight on and continue living in civvy street.

Some of that conditioning can still be useful to you. It's a case of examining your internal toolkit and dropping the things that you don't need now.

I found acceptance to be a powerful tool. I accepted that I'll never really be a civvy again, simply because their values are different and they don't look after each other the way we did when serving. The mates I made in the mob were closer than blood relatives but I had to accept that we were all going our different ways when demobbed and that we may never meet again.

I also had to accept that my condition may not get better because of the complications of my particular journey; I pray that it's not the same for you.

I learned to live with the condition using creative therapies as an outlet and as a means of communicating with the different energies on the Earth. There's a vast well of healing energy there. I use poetry to get my feelings out and photography to connect with the natural energy of the Earth.

I mapped out my good and bad periods and learnt to recognise my cycles. This allows me to prepare for the harder times by taking precautions and working on my spiritual 'self', to keep myself from going under at these difficult periods.

It can sometimes feel like surviving is a full time job because of the energy and effort it takes to cope with the symptoms of PTSD. I had to learn to be kinder to myself and not give myself a bollocking because that doesn't help and just creates division inside of me.

If you get through the day and night and see another sunrise (piss-poor weather aside), congratulate yourself. If you manage to walk away from someone that's pushing your buttons without getting into a physical confrontation with them, reward yourself.

I use catnaps to build up some energy during the day. It compensates for my broken sleep at night.

If you're going for a medical assessment, take someone with you that you trust and please don't feel ashamed of the reactions that the psychiatrist gets out of you. If it's a medical assessment for a war disablement pension or a disability benefit, insist on your companion being with you and ensure that they are making notes about your questions and answers. Accuracy is crucial!

Speak to someone. If you're lucky enough to have supportive partners, family, friends or work colleagues and you feel that they would listen to you without ridiculing or judging you – talk with them! Talking about what happened to you will help clean the wound.

Find a good GP. It may mean trying a few different ones. It's taken me five years to find a decent GP that understands and can empathise with the issues of PTSD. It took two years and a complaint to the NHS before I found a good psychiatrist in the area that has experience of dealing with

PTSD in Veterans. I've given up on Social Services though. See if you can get the Social worker support that you need though.

Remember that if you have a war disablement pension, you are entitled to free prescriptions relating to that disability and that you are also a priority patient for that condition with regard to accessing care through the NHS.

If you need specific care requirements to help you cope with your disability – contact the Rowan Organisation (http://www.therowan.org/)

Head Office

The Rowan Organisation
Eliot Park Innovation Centre
Barling Way
Nuneaton
CV10 7RH

Tel: 02476 322 860
Minicom: 02476 374 439
Fax:02476 374 948

Information Service: 0845 608 8048   Email: info@therowan.org

There is a list of other organisations that can help you toward the end of this book.

If you decide to try using creative therapies to cope with PTSD, you may find some useful information on www.respectip.co.uk - it's an offshoot of my main site which is www.wolf-photography.com. There may be some ideas there that will help you to sell your art.

To Relatives, partners and friends of Veterans

You may not recognise the spirit of the man or woman that returns from an active tour of service. They will be different to the person that you once knew and they will need your care and patience if they've suffered any kind of trauma.

They may not be able to talk about the things that they've experienced and may behave in ways that will be out of character for the person that you knew.

The best thing that you can do is gently encourage them to talk about anything and use that time to build a bridge with them. In time they may open up to you about some of their experiences. I warn you never to push them or to be aggressive in any way toward them, as they will probably disappear from your life and you will have done one of the worst things possible – you will have pushed away someone that needs your love and understanding.

Please remember that if they've recently left the Armed Forces that they may be experiencing difficulties in their readjustment to civvy street. For the time that they served, the services took on the roles of their father, mother, brother and sister. They were conditioned to kill and to give up their lives if necessary in order to carry out their orders.

There's also a very different attitude towards friendship in the Armed Forces: they would have willingly laid down their lives for their brothers and sisters in arms.

At least 25% of homeless people are Veterans. People that have fallen on hard times and found themselves ostracised for their differences; a number of them suffering from PTSD.

15% of the prison population of the UK are Veterans. How many of them are suffering from PTSD? How many of them would not have been sent to prison if their condition, PTSD, was properly diagnosed while they were serving or shortly after their discharge from the services?

Give them the time and space they need but make sure that you see to your own needs as well. Being a carer for a person with a disability can be draining work, emotionally, mentally and physically. You must ensure that you get adequate support for yourself.

You may decide that you need counselling too, as it may allow you time to release any issues building up within or you may get by okay by talking things over with a friend or a relative. It's important for you to be as healthy as possible.

To Professionals working in Mental Health, General Health and Social Work

Working in or areas around Mental Health can be very difficult, and at times - thankless. However, it's an area that you decided to venture into for whatever reason. Most of you will have had some experience of the stresses and strains that life puts on most people. Some of you have experience of mental health problems in your own lives.

I ask you to remember something:

If you don't do your job in a caring, professional way, you will compound the difficulties that Veterans with PTSD face and you will have failed in your duty.

Most Veterans have worked in a professional way and they recognise sloppy work and bad practice.

The reports that you write must be accurate, as you are the people carrying out assessments that will help civil servants decide whether or not a Veteran gets appropriate care and support, as well their War Disablement Pension or equivalent and any other disability benefits that they may be entitled to.

In my experience, it's rare that a person with PTSD will respond aggressively without provocation. When we're asked about our experiences, we often sub-consciously swear. We're not swearing at you though. It's one of the side effects of remembering painful memories and having to recount them to you. You must never threaten to terminate care or support because of someone using bad language – there's a world of difference between someone venting frustration and someone swearing at you. Please recognise the difference and act accordingly.

To The general public

Thank you for buying/reading this and the first title, Words of a Wolf – Poetry of a Veteran. Income from these books and my photography (www.wolf-photography.com) enables me to carry on my 'therapeutic work' and to continue raising awareness of PTSD.

Good luck and look after the 'Self'!

Mitakuye Oyasin
(translates to All My Relations – A Lakota Prayer recognising one's relationship with all living things).

Villayat 'SnowMoon Wolf' Sunkmanitu May 2012.

Also by the author

**Words of a Wolf
Poetry of a Veteran**

Paperback ISBN: 9780956488503
Ebook ISBN: 9780956488558
Kindle ASIN: B0073YE7OQ

The Way of the Wolf – Poetry of a Veteran is also available as:

Ebook ISBN: 9780956488534
Amazon Kindle ASIN: B0084MQIR0

Organisations that can help Veterans

Australia
Department of Veterans' Affairs
(http://www.dva.gov.au/Pages/home.aspx)

Canada
Veterans Affairs Canada (http://www.veterans.gc.ca/eng/)
The Royal Canadian Legion (http://legion.ca/)

UK
Organisations that can help UK Forces Veterans
Combat Stress (http://www.combatstress.org.uk)
Veterans UK (http://www.veterans-uk.info)
The Royal British Legion (http://www.britishlegion.org.uk/)
SSAFA (http://www.ssafa.org.uk/)
RAF Benevolent Fund (http://www.rafbf.org/)
Army Benevolent Fund
http://www.armybenfund.org/index2.html)
Royal Naval Benevolent Trust (http://www.rnbt.org.uk/)
The Gurkha Welfare Trust (http://www.gwt.org.uk/)
NHS mental health support for UK Veterans
(http://www.nhs.uk/Livewell/Militarymedicine/Pages/Veteransmentalhealth.aspx)

USA
Department of Veterans Affairs (http://www.va.gov/)

As a UK Veteran it's worth bearing in mind that the countries above may well be able to help you, if only briefly, by allowing you to talk should you have a bad episode whilst travelling.

Please support this project

Facebook:

http://www.facebook.com/snowmoonwolf

http://www.facebook.com/thewayofthewolf

http://www.facebook.com/wordsofawolf

Twitter:

http://twitter.com/#!/SnowMoonWolf

Main website: http://www.wolf-photography.com

Funds raised from this project will be used to carry out creative work and raise more awareness of how PTSD affects people, particularly Veterans.

If the project makes a profit, some of the funds will be used to purchase materials for the Occupational Therapy unit for Combat Stress to enable other Veterans to use creative arts as a method of coping with PTSD.

Notes